UNCOVER
& DISCOVER

What Has Three Horns and a **Sharp Beak**?

WRITTEN BY **Judy Zocchi**

ILLUSTRATED BY **Russ Daff**

dingles & company New Jersey

First Printing

Published by dingles&company
P.O. Box 508
Sea Girt, New Jersey 08750

**LIBRARY OF CONGRESS
CATALOG CARD NUMBER**
2007929691

ISBN
978-1-59646-820-7

Printed in the United States
of America

The Uncover & Discover series is based on the original concept of Judy Mazzeo Zocchi.

ART DIRECTION & DESIGN
Rizco Design

EDITORIAL CONSULTANT
Andrea Curley

PROJECT MANAGER
Lisa Aldorasi

EDUCATIONAL CONSULTANTS
Melissa Oster and Margaret Bergin

RESEARCH AND ADDITIONAL COPY BY
Robert Kanner

CREATIVE DIRECTOR
Barbie Lambert

PRE-PRESS
Pixel Graphics

WEBSITE
www.dingles.com

E-MAIL
info@dingles.com

The **Uncover & Discover** series encourages children to inquire, investigate, and use their imagination in an interactive and entertaining manner. This series helps to sharpen their powers of observation, improve reading and writing skills, and apply knowledge across the curriculum.

Uncover each one and and see you can when you're

clue one by
what dinosaur
discover
done!

I hatched from a
hard-shelled **egg**.

WHERE IS THE **EGG**?

I have big **eyes** on
either side of my head.
They let me see a wide
view of my surroundings.

LOOK FOR THE **EYE**.

There are **two long, sharp horns** on my brow that I use to defend myself from enemies.

FIND THE TWO LONG, SHARP HORNS.

A **short horn** behind my snout gives me extra protection if I'm threatened.

DO YOU SEE THE **SHORT HORN**?

A large bony plate called a **frill** curves upward behind my head. It protects my neck from the sharp teeth of enemies.

WHERE IS THE **FRILL**?

I have a toothless, parrotlike **beak**. I use it for tearing off mouthfuls of the plants that I eat.

LOOK FOR THE **BEAK**.

My sharp **cheek teeth** can grind up even the toughest plants so I can digest them.

FIND THE CHEEK TEETH.

I can't lift my head very high above the ground, so I eat plants such as **ferns** and shrubs that grow near the ground.

DO YOU SEE THE **FERN?**

I walk slowly
on four short,
sturdy **legs**.

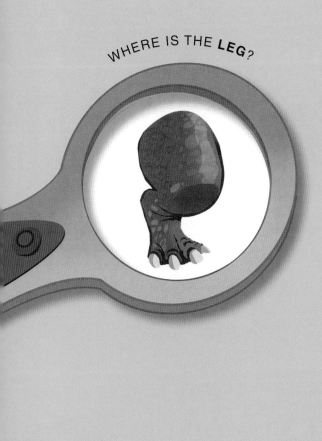

WHERE IS THE **LEG**?

The four **toes** on my
back legs spread out to
help carry my heavy body.

LOOK FOR THE **TOES**.

I have a short,
pointy **tail**.

FIND THE **TAIL**.

Huge, strong **bones**
support my heavy body.

DO YOU SEE THE **BONES?**

You have uncovered the clues. **Have you guessed what I am?**

EGG

EYE

LONG, SHARP HORNS

SHORT HORN

FRILL

BEAK

CHEEK TEETH

FERN

LEG

TOES

TAIL

BONES

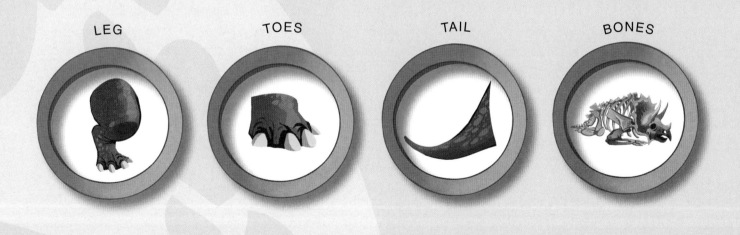

If not, here are more clues.

1. I am a prehistoric reptile that lives on the land.

2. I am the largest of a group of four-legged dinosaurs with horns, a bony frill (a plate that curves upward) behind the head, and a toothless beak with grinding cheek teeth on both sides of my jaw.

3. I have one of the biggest heads of any land animal. It's almost 10 feet long and weighs 600 pounds. That's about the same length and weight as a polar bear!

4. I am about 30 feet long (about the length of a school bus) and about 10 feet tall (about the same height as 2 refrigerators stacked on top of each other).

5. I weigh around 11,000 pounds. That's about the same weight as 20 polar bears together.

6. I walk slowly but will charge at an enemy if threatened.

7. I live in the region that is now the western United States and western Canada.

8. I am a herbivore, which means I eat plants.

Now add them up and you'll see...

I'm a **Triceratops** and you discovered me!

Do you want to know more about me? Here are some *Triceratops* fun facts.

1. *Triceratops* (try-SER-ah-tops) means "three-horned face." The name comes from the three horns sticking out of the dinosaur's head.

2. *Triceratops* lived during the late Cretaceous period, about 72 to 65 million years ago, a time when there were severe climate changes, earthquakes, and volcanic eruptions.

3. Scientists believe that these dinosaurs lived in a herd and kept their young in the center to protect them from enemies.

4. Scientists think *Triceratops* had an excellent sense of smell.

5. *Triceratops* and all other dinosaurs disappeared about 65 million years ago. It is widely believed that a giant asteroid or comet hit Earth and caused major climactic changes to which the dinosaurs couldn't adapt.

6. *Triceratops* was named by Othniel Marsh, a paleontologist (a scientist who learns about prehistoric life-forms by studying fossils), in 1889. He discovered a fossil of a partial skull near Denver, Colorado, in 1887–but thought it was from a buffalo! In 1888 John Bell Hatcher, a professional dinosaur fossil collector, discovered a complete skull in Wyoming. He showed it to Marsh, who then realized that his own fossil was part of a triceratops, not a buffalo.

Who, What, Where, When, Why, and How

USE THE QUESTIONS who, what, where, when, why, and how to help the child apply knowledge and process the information in the book. Encourage him or her to investigate, inquire, and imagine.

In the Book...

DO YOU KNOW WHO named *Triceratops*?

DO YOU KNOW WHAT the featured dinosaur in the book is?

DO YOU KNOW WHERE *Triceratops* lived?

DO YOU KNOW WHEN the first *Triceratops* fossil was discovered?

DO YOU KNOW WHY *Triceratops* ate shrubs that grow near the ground?

DO YOU KNOW HOW many legs *Triceratops* had?

In Your Life...

Scientists believe *Triceratops* lived in herds. How is your family similar to a herd?

CROSS-CURRICULAR EXTENSIONS

Math

Scientists believe that *Triceratops* had about 200 bones. If one scientist found 49 fossilized *Triceratops* bones at a dig site and another scientist found 32 fossilized bones at another dig site, how many more bones would they each have to find in order to make a complete *Triceratops* skeleton?

Science

Scientists believe that the dinosaurs died off about 65 million years ago when a giant asteroid or comet crashed into planet Earth and blocked the sunlight for years. If a giant asteroid or comet hit Earth, what would the effects be on all living creatures?

Social Studies

Triceratops lived in what is now the western United States and western Canada. Name some of the states that are located in the western United States today.

Fun Activity

You have uncovered the clues and discovered *Triceratops*.

ASSIGNMENT
Use your imagination to write a story. Imagine you are a triceratops that just came face-to-face with an enemy.

INCLUDE IN YOUR STORY
Who were you with when you saw your enemy?
What did you do to protect yourself?
Where did your enemy first see you?
When did you notice your enemy?
Why was your enemy a threat to you?
How were you able to defeat your enemy?

WRITE
Enjoy the writing process while you take what you have imagined and write your story.

Author

Judy Zocchi is the creator of the Uncover & Discover series as well as the author of the Global Adventures, Holiday Happenings, Click & Squeak Computer Basics, and Paulie and Sasha series. In addition, she has penned many books under the name of Molly Dingles. Ms. Zocchi is also a lyricist who holds a bachelor's degree in fine arts/theater from Mount Saint Mary's College and a master's degree in educational theater from New York University. She lives in Manasquan, New Jersey.

Illustrator

Since graduating from Falmouth School of Art in 1993, **Russ Daff** has enjoyed a varied career. For eight years he worked on numerous projects in the computer games industry, producing titles for Sony PlayStation and PC formats. While designing a wide range of characters and environments for these games, he developed a strong sense of visual impact that he later utilized in his illustration and comic work. Russ now concentrates on his illustration and cartooning full-time. When he is not working, he enjoys painting, writing cartoon stories, and playing bass guitar. He lives in Cambridge, England.